W9-BBM-407

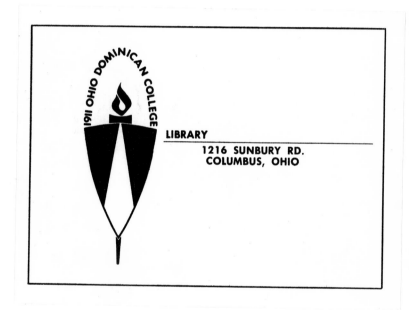

PLAY WITH THE SUN

PLAY WITH THE SUN

Howard E. Smith Jr.

Illustrated by Frank Bozzo

McGRAW-HILL BOOK COMPANY

New York St. Louis San Francisco Auckland Düsseldorf Johannesburg
Kuala Lumpur London Mexico Montreal New Delhi Panama Paris
São Paulo Singapore Sydney Tokyo Toronto

J
523.7
S

Library of Congress Cataloging in Publication Data

Smith, Howard Everett, Jr., date
  Play with the sun.

  SUMMARY: Easy-to-read text suggests activities for
enjoying and learning about the sun.
  1. Sunshine—Juvenile literature. 2. Sun—Juvenile
literature. 1. Sun I. Bozzo, Frank, illus.
II. Title.
QC911.2.S58   523.7   74-26631
ISBN 0-07-059105-9

1234567RABP7898765

For Pat and Ramelle

All winter we look forward to those first warm days of spring
when the leaves come out on the trees,
the flowers bloom, and the birds sing.
At that time everything seems new again.
There are ants, bees, and butterflies.
There are soft clouds drifting in the sky.
We can play outdoors in the bright sunlight
with no coats, hats, or sweaters.
The wind is not harsh and cold any longer.
It is warm and we like to feel the wind as it touches us.
How pleasant the first warm days are!

It is the sun that makes our warm days possible.
The sunlight heats up whatever it touches.
How hot the sun can make things!
Have you ever gone into a closed automobile
that has been parked in the summer sun?
Have you ever walked barefooted across
the hot sands of a lake or sea beach in July?

It can almost hurt, it is so hot.
Have you ever touched one wall in the sunlight
and another one near it which is in the shade?
Have you ever walked on a hot street where the tar
is so soft that it sinks away under your feet and
sticks to your shoes?
If you have done these things
you know how hot the sun can make things.

You can find out that the sun's light is hot—very hot.
One way is to take a magnifying glass
and a piece of paper on a plate that will not burn
that is on the ground far away from any object
which might catch on fire.
Be sure that there is no wind.
Have an adult with you.
Focus the light of the sun onto the paper.
See the little picture of the sun?
Pretty soon the paper will smoke
and then catch on fire.

Have you ever been awake
on a moonless, dark night
and then seen the first light of dawn?
Have you seen the pink light touch the clouds
and watched the trees take shape?
How wonderful it is to see
the daylight return after the darkness
of a long, long night.

We need the light of the sun
so that we can see things
and find our way around.

The sun's light can be very bright,
especially in the middle of the day.
You can try to hide from the sunlight:
Take a table outside,
or even put it inside of a sunny room.
Cover it with blankets and make a little "house."
Go into your "house" and try to make it as dark as you can.
Can you really make it dark? Or is it difficult?

One way that sunlight helps us see things
is that almost everything reflects sunlight.
This means that light bounces off the surface of things.
If you stand with your back to the sun
and look at a wall in front of you,
you will be able to see the wall
because the sunlight bounces off of it.
Very bright things reflect a great deal of light.
Aluminum foil, spoons, and mirrors reflect more light
than black construction paper, soot, or charcoal.

To see some reflections that move,
take a large baking pan and half fill it with water.
Put it near a window in the bright sunlight.
Now stir the water and watch the walls of the room.
You will see beautiful light patterns
move about here and there on the walls.

You can make a hanging light reflector for your window:
From a piece of cardboard make a big cone
as shown in the drawing. Place squares of aluminum
foil on the side of the cone.
Hang the cone from its point in a sunny window by a string.
Now spin the cone and watch the reflected lights.

Have you ever seen sunlight reflected from a window miles away?
Some time, a little before sunset, look at a distant window.
Have your back to the sun. Maybe you'll see window reflections.
The moon does not give off its own light.
The only light you see on it is reflected sunlight,
whether you are looking at it in the daytime or at night.

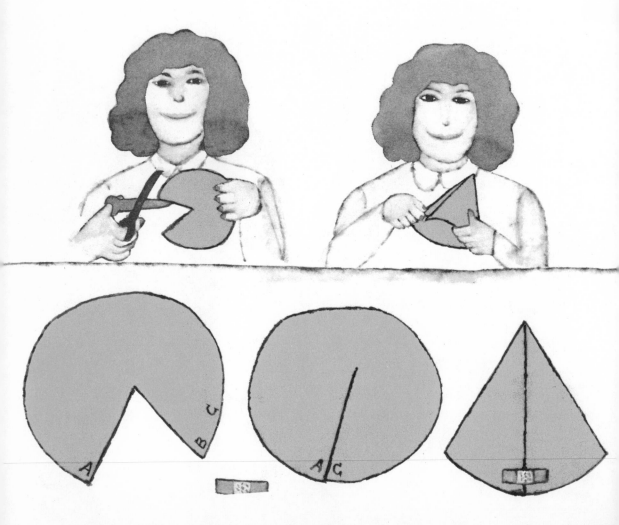

Different things reflect sunlight differently.
A flat hand mirror reflects it one way,
but a big shiny soup spoon reflects it another way.
See how the spoon reflects the sun from inside the spoon
and then see how it reflects it from the back of the spoon.

Look at your image in the spoon
and on the outside too. What happens?

Some light reflections are beautiful.
Many fish scales are, such as those of goldfish.
So are birds' feathers, such as those of a humming bird.
Wet beach or river stones are colorful too. Collect some
stones and keep them in a clear jar with water in it.
Place the jar in a window in the sunlight.

Have you ever gone on a long walk
on a day when there was a thick fog?
Remember how gray everything looked?
The trees looked gray and the houses looked gray.
Then suddenly the wind blew
the fog away and the scene changed.
The trees looked green again and the bricks
of the houses turned bright red.
When the sun comes out the whole world changes.
Everything has much more color to it.

You do not need a cloudy day to see this:
Go into a room full of sunlight.
Pull down all of the windowshades or blinds.
How dull all the colors become!
Let the shades go up again and
watch the colors as the sunlight flows in again.

You can make objects which really become brilliant
when the sunlight touches them.
For instance, fill little, clear bottles with water.
Add a little red, blue, or yellow food coloring to the water.
You can get food coloring at any large grocery store.
The colors are used to color cookies and other pastries.

Place your bottles on a windowsill
where the sunlight can touch them.
Look at them on dull, cloudy days,
and also on bright, sunny days. How brilliant they can be!

Jewelry gleams more in the sunlight, too.
Snow shimmers and twinkles in sunlight.
So do dewdrops on grass early in the morning.
If you have plants such as geraniums in the window,
see how the leaves and flowers
become more colorful when
the sun shines through them.

Sometimes when there is a shower
the sun will come out, and a rainbow will appear
briefly on a large, dark, rain cloud.
Where do the colors of the rainbow come from?
Certainly they don't come from the gray cloud.
The rainbow's colors come from the sunlight.
Sunlight itself has colors in it which our eyes see.
All the drops of water in a cloud break up the light
and separate out the colors of the sunlight.

Rainbows are rare, but you can make a rainbow
which will be all your own to play with.
Get a garden hose and turn on the water so that you get
a fine spray coming out of the nozzle.
Do it on a bright sunny day. Turn your back toward the sun
and look at the spray. Hold it high. See the rainbow?
It is exactly like a rainbow seen in a big rain cloud.

You can actually find rainbow colors
in many places.
Most streets have oily spots on them.
When the streets get wet, some oil floats on the water.
After a rainfall, stand on a sidewalk and look at the street.
You can often find little wet spots
that have rainbow colors in them.

You can have rainbows indoors as well,
ones which you can play with.
Take a small hand mirror and place it
in a pan of water as shown in the drawing.
Put the pan and mirror in a window in strong sunlight.
Watch the walls of the room for your rainbow.

When the sun's light is stopped, we get shadows.
You can easily block the light and get shadows of the sun.
Some bright sunny day stand on a sidewalk or some paved area.
Put your arms out and block the rays of the sun.
See your shadow? Wave your arms.
See your shadow wave back at you?
Your shadow does whatever you want it to!
The only thing is, you can't get rid of it.
You cannot tell it to go away.

If you stood in one spot all day and watched your shadow,
you would see that in the early morning it was really long.
At around noontime it would be much shorter,
especially in the summertime,
and then late in the afternoon your shadow would be long again.
Your shadow will also move all day.

The sun appears to move all of the time.
In the morning the sun rises and starts crossing the sky.
All day long it seems to move across the sky and finally sets.
In the morning, sunlight may be in some rooms of your home,
but in the afternoon the same rooms may have no sunlight at all.
Watch how the light in rooms changes during the day as
sunlight goes from room to room in your home.

The sun seems to move in the sky, but does it really move?
No, actually the sun does not move at all.
It is the earth we live on that actually moves all of the time.
It only looks as though the sun moves across the sky.

When you ride in a car things outside the car windows
seem to move by you all the time.
But of course you know that they do not move.
You know that it is the car that is moving.
Stand in the center of a room
and take a mailing tube or roll up a paper
and put it to your eye and look through it.
Now slowly turn around and around.
The room and things in it seem to move.
Because the earth moves, the sun seems to move in the sky.

But how does the earth move?
It is spinning around and around like a top
or like an apple hanging from a string.
You can easily spin an apple. Tie a string to the stem of one
and let it spin around and around.
Hold it in a room with only one light on.
Now spin the apple. Notice how some of the apple is in the light
and some of the apple is in the dark.
If you were very, very small like a bug and lived on the apple,
you would see the light move. You would see it rise and set.
It would be very much like seeing the sun rise and set.
As the earth spins, we have day and night, one after the other.

How fast does the sun and its shadows move?
When you look at some shadows made by the sun, for a minute or two
they do not seem to move.
But they move faster than you might think.
Take a piece of paper and put it in the sunlight, indoors.
Place a pencil upright inside of an empty threadspool.
Notice the shadow of the pencil. Mark the shadow.
Does it move? In a few minutes? In an hour?
Look at the shadow mark until you notice it move.
The shadow moves as the sun seems to move across the sky.
If the earth moved faster, would the shadows move faster?

One can tell time with moving shadows.
Long before people had clocks, they had sundials.
A sundial marks a moving shadow of the sun,
and one can tell time with it.
You can make a sundial for yourself:
Put a tall stick in the ground,
where the ground is flat, wide, and clean.
Take a clock or watch. Every hour mark where the
sun's shadow is. Write down the time next to the shadow.
On the next clear, sunny day go out and watch the shadows
touch your hour marks. You can tell the time with them.
You have made a sundial. Most sundials have mottos.
You can write one on yours, perhaps one used centuries ago:
"I count only the sunny hours."

Have you ever watched the sunlight
move through the dust of a dusty room,
or move through the dirty water of a lake,
or move through campfire smoke in a forest?
If you have, you have seen light rays,
or as some people call them, sunbeams.
These are lines of light which come from the sun.
Many pictures of the sun show these rays.
It is fun to draw pictures of the sun and show
sunbeams coming from it.
You can see the sunbeams from the sun:
Take a glass of water, add a few drops of milk to it,
and place a piece of black paper all around the glass.
Make a small hole in the black paper
and let the sun shine through the hole.
Look down into the glass from the top.
You can see the light rays.
Each ray moves in a straight line.

The sun's rays touch things differently.
Some day look at the east wall of a house.
In the morning the sun's rays hit it directly.
A few minutes before noon, however,
the sun will not shine directly on the wall.

Then the sun's rays will slant across the wall,
just barely touching it.
When the sun's rays slant across the wall one can see
all sorts of little shadows on it.
You might also see cracks, bumps, and paint chips on the wall.
You could not see them as well before.
Now they are clear, sharp, and easy to see.

You do not have to wait for the sun to move to see
how different things can be lit by the sun's rays.
Take a slice of white bread out into the sunlight.
Let the sun's rays shine on it directly
and look at the piece of bread. How white it *all* looks.
Now turn it sideways so the sunlight just glances across the bread.
Now you can clearly and easily see all the holes in the bread.
Notice other things this way. Turn the palm of your hand
in sunlight. Look at it with direct light and slanting light.
See how different it looks. See the lines of your hand.
Take rocks, leaves, knitted things, like sweaters,
and look at them in the same way.

Not only can shadows change in direct and slanting light, but
they change a great deal in soft and bright light.
On clear, bright days shadows are sharp and dark.
On gray, cloudy days they become soft.
If you make a shadow screen
you can see interesting lights and shadows
during the day when the sun is shining.
Take a shallow box and take the cover off of it.
Cut out holes in the bottom of the box.
Some of them can be triangles, squares, or other designs.
Over the open top, place a tight piece of white tissue paper.
Hang the box up in a window where the sun shines.
Be sure that the holes are against the window
and that the side with the tissue paper is in the room.
When the sun is bright there will be sharp designs
on the tissue paper; when it is gray and cloudy outside
the shadows will be much softer.
To make it even more interesting
place colored pieces of cellophane over some of the holes.

1

2

One important thing about the sun
is that trees, flowers, seaweed—all plants—
need the sun so that they can live.
You have seen how the leaves fall
off of the trees in the autumn
and grow back in the springtime,
when the sunny days are warmer.

You can easily have a plant of your own
to take care of and to watch.
You can buy a small geranium
and let it grow indoors near a sunny window.
It is an easy plant to grow
and it has pretty, colorful flowers.
All year it is fun to watch plants change.

There are many ways of playing
with the sun.
You can play with it either all day long
or all year long
and find out how it changes and what it does.

ABOUT THE AUTHOR AND ARTIST

Howard E. Smith, Jr. has written magazine articles, the narration for a children's film, and several children's books, including PLAY WITH THE SUN. He worked for Don Herbert, the "Mr. Wizard" of TV and, for a number of years, has been a children's science book editor.

A graduate of Colorado College, Mr. Smith now lives in Brooklyn, New York with his wife and two children.

Frank Bozzo spends many afternoons chasing shadows in the park besides teaching illustration at the School of Visual Arts in New York, where he studied. Mr. Bozzo has illustrated numerous children's books including: HERMAN'S HAT, THE WAY THE TIGER WALKED, and THE BEASTS OF NEVER. He is the winner of many awards both nationally and from the Society of Illustrators, the Art Director's Club of New York, and the American Institute of Graphic Arts.

Mr. Bozzo, his wife and three children live in New New York City.

95972